WATCH WORDS

Thoughts on Race, Water and War

by
Beatrice Perry Soublet

edited by Kathryn V. Stanley

authorHOUSE®

AuthorHouse™
1663 Liberty Drive, Suite 200
Bloomington, IN 47403
www.authorhouse.com
Phone: 1-800-839-8640

First published by AuthorHouse 11/25/2008

ISBN: 978-1-4389-2081-8 (sc)

Library of Congress Control Number: 2008908891

Printed in the United States of America
Bloomington, Indiana

This book is printed on acid-free paper.

DEDICATION

To those who held on through the storm
To those who have inspired the poet in me

February 1, 1992.

Dear Beatrice,
     With best wishes to
my Colleague — who
has learned what it takes
to survive the 'Whirlwind!
Again! — hold on!
               Love,
          Gwendolyn Brooks.
          February 1, 1992.

MIDDLE PASSAGE REVISITED

Forgive me, for not laboring with you
over the historic sadness of our crossing.

Forgive me *for* not reliving the pain,
Not weeping fresh tears over the dead
    who perished at sea.
And not lamenting the unequalled brutality
    that we suffered at the hands of our masters.

I've heard that story often enough.
I've gone back to the well of tears
    that I dredge up at the sight
    of the slave-mother's wrenching
     from her life's blood;
    Tom from her man
     and made her master's plaything.

I've heard and reheard the loud wail
    of the beaten and tortured slave.

I've sung and resung the sorrow songs,
    and praised to the end the joyful slave,
    who believes as do I
     that "there's a brighter day a comin',
    Hallelu and Hallelu!"

But what I want to know is,
Now that we've made it across
     and made it through,
     will we make it over?

Will we find a level of greatness
     that will prove us the people of spirit
       that we have always been?

Will we stop imitating our oppressors
     and buying into the empty values
     that are the ruination of the American culture?

Will we stop pumping filth into our veins,
     heads and hearts?

Did we come this far to perish?

WEIGHED IN THE BALANCE

A people driven to respond

Left on foreign shores

Broken—a part of a long history of pain and suffering

Too few allies

Alien songs sung by enemies

Drums no more

Created language

Cultivated at the heart of a molded field

Driven by misery

Cultivated by greed

A country, weighed in the balance and found wanting

Slavery

America

AFRICA

Raped mother
Torn from children
Resources stolen
No thought of consequences
Come home to the heart
Give back what was stolen
Created monsters
Stealing from people
Bad lessons learned well
Pain, misery, our mother,
Crying, burning dying
We must help
Go back home
Find your way
Walk over the edge of vanity
Throw away longings
Put back stolen treasures
Walk back, give back
MOTHER cries, MOTHER longs
MOTHER dies as do we

RACE AND WATER

Come high water.
Drown out the hopes and cries,
The needs and desires of the poor, the dark
The water has been high for years.
The foundation shifting,
The green space going,
The people have been endangered for centuries
Drifting, floating, drowning,
Abandoned by Union soldiers
Abandoned by Andrew Johnson,
Abandoned, left to sink,
Decorating southern trees,
Scorched, burning, manhood taken.
High water, flood stage,
Levees always endangered.
Leave 'em, let them sink
Leave 'em, let them drown.
They are not ours.
Leave them.

WATERMARK

It's still there

You can see it on the sides of the houses

Where it came

Where it stayed

Where it waited

Carrying away our hearts; Carrying away our dreams

Giving us a need for safety

Not for the hard lessons of preparation

Nothing of planning overflowed

No one knew and said it

The mark is still there

How high did it go?

How high was it all going to go?

All the way to the White House

The watermark is still there

Bodies floated; babies cried,

Hungry people wanted water, safety, assurance

The watermark is still there

Still a ring; a mark on our hearts, in our minds

A FORGOTTEN CITY

A FORGOTTEN PEOPLE

ORGANIZE

We need a group, a nameless group

Task unwritten

But task known

Change the dynamics

Find the lesson

Teach the agenda

Argue with the powerful

Strip away the lies

Bring in the experts

Fix it

Where are the "National Associations of Black This and That"?

What are they doing, nothing?

Where are we going to go?

What can we do to fix it?

Where is the help?

We dyin' out here

We not survivin'

We dyin'

Where is the help?

Where's the "National Association of Black This and That"?
Where are the big car people?
The big house people?
Where are our people to help us?
We dyin' out here
What chawll waitin' fo'?

NOT THE SAME

Time was, we knew what would be next
Or at least so we thought
Time was, each day brought something expected
Something remembered
Experienced
Something remembered
We knew
Time was, we had a sense of what would be
Or thought we did
Then it all changed
The big water came
Washed away what we knew
Washed out what we thought
Time was, we thought we knew
Then the big water came
And we are not the same

LAST WATCH

Come look at the morning
Silently and bravely it creeps across the sky;
People who hope for light
Wait anxiously on rooftops,
Hoping for the sound of helicopters
Waiting for the sound of hope
A bottle of water
A blanket to put over mama
She left us yesterday
One more day of waiting
The last watch
The water is around us
The last watch
Waiting for a rescue from a storm that wouldn't stop
A storm of neglect, racism, ineptitude
Abandonment
The last watch
Send us a boat, a ship
Send us a Marshall Plan
Can I just get a bottle of clean water?
The last watch for America, USA

DIASPORA

Call yo' mama
Get some sugar from yo' neighbor
Where's the neighbor with the eggs
Gone
All gone
What to do?
Where to find them?
Diaspora
Call yo' mama on the phone
No dial tone
Call yo' daddy
He's in Mt. Olivet
No dial tone
No connection
Diaspora
Where's the remnant
Come on home y'all
Go back y'all.
Where's the remnant?
Start it up again
Diaspora—Remnant
Twins gone to other corners
Who wins? No one.

Diaspora

Remnant

Who wins

No one

Home Go home

Diaspora, remnant sad

Sad

Come back

Go back

Remake

Rebuild

Remnant

Diaspora

Shine somewhere else

MISSING HOME

When will it be back?
When will it sing again?
People are trying
People are home
Where am I?
Why not there in the struggle?
A deserter
Missing in Action, MIA
Gone from the struggle
Gone from my home
Where the heart is
Where is the heart?
Home is where?
Home is where the heart longs to be
Home is the heart
The heart is always
Home
Missing
Missing in Action
Missing home

SCATTERED

So far away from each other
Too far to see or talk
Too much to do to get back
Too far away from what we can give
Too sad
No one to walk with
No one to cry with
Scattered
Strength dissipated
Scattered craft, art
All gone away
Scattered-not wanting to be what we were
Not able to be what we were
Too much to feel
To really think and feel
Scattered forces
Scattered dreams, hopes, visions

WALKING THROUGH WATER

At the other side of the river you stand
Waiting for something, someone to come,
A boat, a raft
Someone, with something
You wade out
The water seems warm
Seems inviting
You find a path
Only a narrow one
FOLLOW IT
STAY ON IT
You will not sink
Others have gone there
Others have made it
STAY ON IT
Don't wait for a raft or a boat
WALK OUT ON YOUR OWN

TOO DEEPLY

Only one cup

Only one cup

From which we all drink the same water

Used and reused

Too little restraint

Too much filtered through

The same water

Only one cup

We drink too deeply

We fill our waterholes

Our extremely busy lives

Our empty hearts

We drink too deeply

Our souls are athirst

FEED MY SHEEP

For the Homeless

Cold and lonely,

Out on the street

Without hope or health, your **father** sat.

His eyes were empty.

Remember when he protected you?

Cold and lonely

Out on the street

Without hope or health, your **mother** sat

Her hands were withered.

Remember when she cared for you?

Cold and lonely,

Out on the street,

Without hope or health, your **brother** sat.

His feet were bleeding.

Remember when he played with you?

Cold and lonely,

Out on the street,

Without hope or health, **you** sat.
Your eyes were empty.
Your hands were withered
Your feet were bleeding:
Remember.

THE WATER'S COLD

Dip just one finger in

It's cold, but not unwelcoming.

Standing at the edge will only make you sad.

Wade in

Just a little at first

Too much to overcome

But start with a finger

Then maybe your hand—

It's cold but not uninviting

Cold is good

Wake up to the coolness

Walk out into the branch of hope

STANDING DOWNSTREAM

All that we placed
All that we used
All that we waste
Follows us –too few will try
Many wander and watch
Writhing in pain
Animals drink
Downstream
All that we use
Flowing out
Flowing down
Too much is unclear
Too many dying
At home in no world
An enemy of the planet

THE GHOST SHIP

Waiting at the side of the river
On the banks of a dead sea
At the helm of the ghost ship, was a man
A good man but a man
One who sat at the place where no one wanted to be
Looking for the ghost ship
Waiting for the hollow sound of the bell
Longing to ring but not able
The horn
The empty hold
Calling back from the edge of sanity
Preferring to stay on the other side

WAITING FOR MIRACLES

A few people remembered
A time long before now
A place foreign to this one
Found at the corner of memory
Locked against strange intrusion
Captured in memory
Catapulted into open space
Miracles that came regularly
Opening a soul lost in sadness
Miracles-great and small
They came as we waited, watched, remembered,
believed, watched
A miracle awaits

WAIT AT THE EDGE

The older gentleman watched

As too many who would not wait, swam away.

Gone after hopes, dreams, promises

That would not come true

Would not open

Standing at the garden of flowers

That would only bud, never bloom

Waiting at the open grave

Hearts torn

Rendered hopeless and powerless

The older gentleman knew

The pain and disappointment of waiting

He found it obvious and evident

It wasn't at all a sad thing

He knew

He had waited at the edge before

Too many people were unyielding-not remembering

But he knew.

WAITING FOR WISDOM

Standing on the side of sanity
Waiting for one clear thought
Waiting for someone to explain
The side that didn't make sense
Standing on the side of sanity
The voice that would not speak
    whispered inside the thoughts of a sad man.
A man who wasn't at the helm
    when the ship crashed
But knew it would
Wisdom came in a moment of clarity
A vision of necessity
Walking on the water of sanity from the other side

FROZEN LONGINGS

The heart of a truly kind person
Frozen in the epicenter
Frozen at the force
Frozen by some who would let it be
The heart of the original ones was left to melt
Left to be tended by only a sharp edged tool.
Left to see what would come of the melting
Edged out by a willing heart
One that would not be broken
Frozen, then set out on the ice floe with the old ones
Of no more use
Set out to wait for death
It did not come quickly
The hearts of the pure, the kind the loved ones do not break easily
The frozen area of life is only cold to those who go there.
Watching as they drift by
Open to all possibilities
Too drunk with passion to see a future
Waiting for the end
Still beating, still, waiting, watching, wanting

PRESSURE

Too deep and hard and over the top
Pushing down to make sure nothing stops
Too much to think of
Too much to let go
Press down, push out
Hold on sides, explode
Put your hand on his heart
While it pumps
While it explodes
Don't go
Don't leave
Keep pushing don't go
Don't leave
Don't disappear
Disaster is at the heart of your pressure
Press down, overflow
Don't leave-stay
I'll press

PEACE

Like rain that falls at intermittent places
Like New Orleans rain that falls on one block and not another
Peace falls on those who least need, hope for or expect it
Peace falls on the just, peace falls.
But do they receive it?
Peace comes in forms not seen or recognized
When not searching, peace comes like a rain that comes at a time of
trust and sadness
A time of joy, labor, and hope but we don't see it
Because we don't expect it

PEACE TALKS

Come to the table
Bring your heart
Open, willing
Trust that I will speak
Trust that I will listen
Trust that I will hear
Come to the table
Bring your heart
Open, willing
Not in despair
Not destroyed
No brokenness
Bring you heart
Trust that I will help, heal
Bring your heart
Bare, open
Trust me.
I trust you

MORTIFIED

Free at last

Free at last

Free to kill

To imitate

To annihilate

Free at last

Turn on my brother

Turn on my sister

Turn on myself

Free at last

Free to kill

Free to hate

Free to sell ourselves

Free at last

What about Frederick, Harriet, Denmark, John Brown?

What about the "Glory" soldiers?

What about Martin?

After all they did.

Shame on us

Kill the legacy

Shoot the dream

Deafened by noise of bling

Sing against order
Sing against respect
Sing against women
Free at last
Disappearing dad
Free to go
Free to make and leave
Spread your seed like glue
Sticking to everyone but yourself
Free at last
Lay down with anybody
Spread for anybody
Free at last to annihilate ourselves

CROCK POT

Full of moldy ideas
Cooking at a low temperature
Cooking at a slow speed
Thoughts, ruminations
Heating slowly
Smells of rot filling our nostrils
Adding the seasonings
        of
Stupidity, Lack of Foresight, Injustice,
Unequal Distribution of Wealth

A crock pot full of pain, misery
Cooking at a low temperature
Bubbles that were overwhelming
A sign of ruin
Don't eat it
Start over
Pour it out
Wash the pot
Start over.

DRY WELL

Attached to his heart was nothing that worked
A good pump attached to a dry well.
Found at the edge of what had been a working device
But now no one remembered when,
    Where or how it would ever have worked.
Attached to a working heart was a dry well
Nothing to give
Working—but for no purpose—
Who would recognize anyone at the cage?
Found by a lost person
Too gruesome to make a good tale
A pump attached to a dry well.
A heart attached to an empty soul.
Someone would know, recognize, help
Someone could see just enough to help
Recognize what could have been, what had been
Help clear the path.

AT THE WELL

I'm going to stand at the well
And wait for what I want to hear
The sound of water running out of the dark
A deep sound
Throw a pebble in
Wait for the sound

LOW POINT

Not at the bottom but near,
    The bottom is in sight.
Right at the round, smooth part
Right at the part where if you stretched out
    your feet you could touch it.

But the bottom is also the best place to push up from
Pushing up toward the top
Pushing off
Using the bottom as a launching point
A point from which to get back on top
Bouncing back up
Pushing off from the bottom
Bouncing off, up
Pushing
Launching from the low point
Stretching out-
Pushing up from the bottom

Moving toward
Stretching out
Bouncing up
Bouncing back
Low point
Launching pad
Remember

DANCE AND WAR

That's the sound of the drum
The call of the drums
Dance to the drum
Is that the guns?
Is that the drum
Dance to the fun
Dance to the drum
Death dance
Harsh steps
Move to the side
Dodge, dance
Jump, fly, fall
Dance to the drum
Dance to the gun
Dance for death

NOT RUN IN VAIN

That seems like a plan
Waiting to see how it went
Waiting to see the effect of her words
Wanting to hear only good reports
Unwilling to concede defeat
Not at the heart of the matter
Only on the fringes of reason
But certain that a plan would come
Watching at the gate of wisdom
Waiting for some semblance of reason
A promise, a hope that she had not run in vain
Any attempt to bring about change
Any desire to fix all that is broken
Can be seen from a great distance
Distressed hearts wake up
 on the shore of hopelessness
The battlefield is strewn with the souls of people
 who did not find a path to peace
What is the correct metaphor for peace?
Battle weary, we turn and wait

Have we run in vain?

WAR

When did it start that we can't settle things at a table?

A round table

A table of peace

A table of the heart

When did it start that we can't talk?

That life is so cheap

That we can't talk

That it is either them or us, not we

When did it start that we can hurt children?

Destroy their schools, their water?

When did it start?

When will it end?

BATTLEFIELD

Who stands at the edge looking down
   in the abyss of despair?
Not remembering when things were better
Looking at the enemy of peace
Making stone-faced response
   to gestures of good will
Standing, resting, weary from the battle of words,
    Wills and weapons
Not capable of hearing
   The battle cry
Unwilling to speak for or to peace
Looking for someone who would speak
A voice clear enough to make keening
Come away from the edge
Look out and up
Find a point of focus that is rich
   And warm and welcoming
Make a peace pact with the poisonous tyrant
   who eats the flesh of goodness
Watch, wait
See a time when your words of wisdom nd peace
will be heard

Start speaking now.

ISLAND OF HOPE

Stand at the gate and watch
See if anyone comes
Wait in joyful expectation
Know that it is in waiting
That joy comes
In hoping that joy is fulfilled
Stand on the Island of Hope
Surrounded by doubters and naysayers
Bring in the Phantom of Peace
Wait for the heart of darkness to fail
Bring in the lamp of goodness
A new day
Convinced of your power
Make all right with you.

JUST BEFORE

Before there was time
For another idea
He walked away
Staring at stars
Not looking at anyone in particular
See the outside
See the underside
The lost refuge of the oppressed
Looking at himself as the answer
But not remembering why
The opening event in a closing show
Just before the ending of the opening
He died.

LEVELING

Bringing in the most evident examples

Parting with the extremes

Bringing down the most evident opposition

Parting with excess

Dropping the pretense of ownership

Dropping the example of richness

Giving it all back

Not some

Not a little

But all

Not using too much

Not draining the cup

Bringing it to the altar from whence it came

Blessed,

Broken

Shared

TIDBITS OF HOPE

Standing at the shore
The kind ones wait for the ship
Holding in their hands baskets of joy, peace, hope, love
Ready and willing to throw them.
Throw them into the raging water
Standing close enough to be harmed
Drowned, destroyed, but not afraid
Willing to risk
Willing to wait, to watch for anyone
To show them that spot
But they must find it themselves
Throw the tidbits
All together
Creating a calmness
A proof of goodness within the raging current

UNEQUAL PEACE

Standing on the bank of freedom
The slave watched his master die
He held tight to the reins
The horses stumbled
The carriage fell
The master crushed beneath the wheels
Finding no part in his heart for pity, shame, sadness
He walked away
Leaving horse, carriage, master
    To survive, die on their own.

Left them as he had so often been left
    By those who would stab him
Left to work
Left to want
Left to starve
He left them
"Good fo' y'all!"

COOL PEACE

Troubled hearts
Troubled spirits
Cleansed by just this
Washed by just this
A calm breath
A wind
A cooling hand
A place of respite
A cool pond of freedom

THE HIGH SAINT

Watching at the gate of remorse
A saint will stand
Waiting for the opportunity to enter
I saw her, the prophet-saint
Saying her "Thus saieth the Lords"
   To those who are deaf
Speaking her admonitions at the gate of despair
Hoping to rouse a few
Hoping to remind a few to leave the altars,
the temple , the mosques, and "go ye therefore"
   So send I you

Waiting at the gate of indifference
The prophet gives a hearty farewell
   To all who would venture out and leave
Leave the comfort, the warmth, the certainty
   of today for the hope of tomorrow,
   and the promise of all time
Go ye therefore
So send I you.

Go

HOMEY, GO HOME!

Go chill in front of your house.
Watch your brothers and sisters
Walkin' in front of yo' crib, pad, personal living space.
See they pants
They drawers
They tattoos
Listen to they music
Stand on the corner for just a day.
Watch they commercial interactions
See they deals goin' down.
Wait at the intersection of some old dream
Long ago dreamed by
Frederick, W.E.B., Sojourner, Daisy.
Homey, Go Home
Go back to Carter G.
Listen to him.
Sit on the porch with Frederick
Ask him 'bout his hair
Let him tell you about his heart.
Homey , go home
See the lamplight

See them reading by secret,
By night.
Under the porch
Afraid
Finger missin', caught readin'
Homey, Go Home
Yo' kinfolk is waitin' for you.

UNEXPECTED CONSEQUENCES

Not knowing which way it would fall
A young man pulled on a vine
   and found himself ensnared in a
rosebush
It had grown high above the ground
Not at eye level
Not where he had looked
Not where he had expected it
Not where he had hoped
But high above the ground, the thorns overtook him
The petals seemed weak indeed
He didn't see any beauty or color
Just ensnared by vine and thorn
None came to free him
He was not able to work his way out
So be waited and in the waiting, came a peace
And in the peace came a vision.

EVIL IN THE TEMPLE

The righteous stand outside
Waiting for the right moment to cleanse the temple
Waiting for the right moment to call for a change
The pure wait for the wind to change
Wait for the evidence of the others to make their case
Standing and waiting,
    the time comes and passes,
      for them to enlighten others

Bring forward the evidence of wisdom and richness
Bring forward the proof of piety
Let it resound from the essence
Let it come to the forefront
Do not stand and wait outside
The cleansing of the temple
    is the essence of your work.

Go in now, do not wait.

There will be no good time.

TIME OUT

Your brother, slow of speech
hesitant of step
Walks down the long hall
Gurney waiting
Can you go –can you walk also?
Days, month, years before
Defended by a somnolent lawyer
A misinformed jury deliberated
Revenge, race, poverty danced together
Your brother takes the walk down the long hall.
Slow of speech, hesitant of step
We all wait at the gurney.
We all mix the lethal cocktail.
We all administer the poison.
A piece of us dies with him.
TIME OUT

DOWN THE MIDDLE

Right in the center of the stream
Where no one bothered to look
A few lilies floated
Too far from shore some thought
To be really strong
But still they floated
Attached to strong roots
Reaching the muddy bottom
They showed what real beauty was
Unattached to anything visible
Floating like pictures of flowers on water
Painted by an artist long gone
They were suspended floating—out of touch—untouched
We are like them, rooted but unattached
Seeming to float—
No apparent struggle
Too far from shore to be touched
Attractive to those who will look
But alone in our own beauty.
Not needing human approval.
No affirmation of our beauty required.

ALWAYS BRING YOUR SUNGLASSES

You may not need them
Not right away.
But bring your sunglasses
A promise of sun will be fulfilled
You can remember better times
Shinier time
Warmer days
Salutary times
Remind yourself of the brightness
Look at you glasses and remember
Light is never far away
Gloom endures for a night
Light always returns in the morning
Each sunrise is different, new
Refreshing the heart.
A reminder that each day brings a bright new chance
Bring your sunglasses
You will always need them.

ABOUT THE AUTHOR

Beatrice Perry Soublet is a poet and retired educator from New Orleans, Louisiana who migrated to Atlanta, Georgia after Hurricane Katrina. A graduate of Bennett College, Soublet is active in the anti-war movement and facilitates a multi-racial discussion group called Erace. She is also a member of the NAACP and has worked with N'COBRA. Soublet's previous works include: The Grinning Darkie and Screams from a Silent African. Her short story titled Roots Woman appeared in Callaloo. Her literary and civic contributions have been honored by her sorority, Delta Sigma Theta Sorority, Inc. and the Amistad Research Center. Married and the mother of two adult children, Soublet is a member of Our Lady of Lourdes Catholic Church.

ABOUT THE EDITOR

Kathryn V. Stanley is an attorney, freelance writer and editor living in East Point, Georgia. Her writing has appeared in various publications including, Essence, Emerge and Black Issues Book Review magazines. She previously served as editor of the faith section of Black Issues Book Review. She has worked with a number of well- known authors and publishers. She is the proud daughter and soror of Beatrice Perry Soublet.